D0844239

CONNECTICUT

by Jim Mezzanotte

GARETH**STEVENS**
GS
PUBLISHING
A Member of the WRC Media Family of Companies

Please visit our web site at: **www.garethstevens.com**
For a free color catalog describing Gareth Stevens Publishing's
list of high-quality books and multimedia programs, call
1-800-542-2595 (USA) or 1-800-387-3178 (Canada).
Gareth Stevens Publishing's fax: (877) 542-2596.

Library of Congress Cataloging-in-Publication Data

Mezzanotte, Jim.
 Connecticut / Jim Mezzanotte.
  p. cm. — (Portraits of the states)
 Includes bibliographical references and index.
 ISBN-10: 0-8368-4663-X ISBN-13: 978-0-8368-4663-8 (lib. bdg.)
 ISBN-10: 0-8368-4682-6 ISBN-13: 978-0-8368-4682-9 (softcover)
 1. Connecticut—Juvenile literature. I. Title. II. Series.
 F94.3.M49 2006
 974.6—dc22   2005044481

Updated edition reprinted in 2007. First published in 2006 by
Gareth Stevens Publishing
A Weekly Reader Company
1 Reader's Digest Rd.
Pleasantville, NY 10570-7000 USA

Editorial direction: Mark J. Sachner
Project manager: Jonatha A. Brown
Editor: Catherine Gardner
Art direction and design: Tammy West
Picture research: Diane Laska-Swanke
Production: Jessica Morris and Robert Kraus

Picture credits: Cover, © Paul J. Stiephaudt; pp. 4, 18, 22, 27, 29 © Mae
Scanlan; p. 5 © Painet; pp. 6, 10 © North Wind Picture Archives; p. 8 © Corel;
p. 9 Library of Congress; p. 12 © Peter Stackpole/Time & Life Pictures/Getty
Images; pp. 15, 16, 24, 25, 26 © Gibson Stock Photography; p. 20 © Don
Eastman; p. 28 © Jim McIsaac/Getty Images

Printed in the United States of America

2 3 4 5 6 7 8 9 10 09 08 07

CONTENTS

Words that are defined in the Glossary appear
in **bold** the first time they are used in the text.

On the Cover: Many of Connecticut's rivers flow into Long Island Sound.
The sound is part of the Atlantic Ocean.

Introduction

If you visited Connecticut, what would you do? Climb aboard an old ship at Mystic Seaport? See dinosaur bones at the Yale Peabody Museum? Take a walk on a sandy beach? The state has many fun places to visit.

Connecticut is the third smallest state in the nation. But don't let its size fool you! The state has played a big part in U.S. history. Important ideas about government started here. Two presidents lived in this state. Its **factories** have made many supplies for U.S. soldiers.

The state has busy cities and quiet, pretty towns. It also has beautiful forests, lakes, and beaches. Connecticut is a small state with a lot to offer!

At Mystic Seaport, you can see old ships, such as this whaling ship.

4

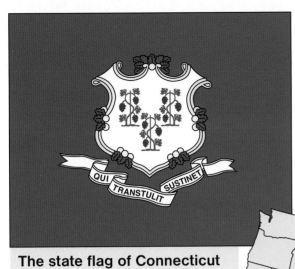

The state flag of Connecticut

CONNECTICUT FACTS

- Became the 5th U.S. State: January 9, 1788
- Population (2006): 3,504,809
- Capital: Hartford
- Biggest Cities: Bridgeport, New Haven, Hartford, Stamford
- Size: 4,845 square miles (12,548 square kilometers)
- Nicknames: Constitution State, Nutmeg State
- State Tree: White oak
- State Flower: Mountain laurel
- State Animal: Sperm whale
- State Bird: American robin

History

Native Americans first settled in the Connecticut area thousands of years ago. They lived in the Connecticut River Valley. They also lived along the coast of Long Island Sound. They grew corn and other crops. They fished and hunted, too.

The First Europeans

Adriaen Block was the first European in Connecticut. He was Dutch. In 1614, he sailed along the shoreline. Then, he went up the Connecticut River. He traded with the Native people. Later, the Dutch built a fort near the river. They did not build any lasting settlements in the area.

In 1633, English people arrived. They came from a nearby **colony** called Plymouth. Plymouth had strict laws.

At first, Natives helped colonists in Connecticut. Later, the two groups fought. In this picture, colonists attack a Pequot village in 1637.

The Pequot Massacre

Natives and colonists did not always get along. At first, Natives helped the colonists. Later, the two groups fought about the land. The colonists thought they owned the land. The Natives thought everybody shared it. In 1637, colonists attacked a village of Pequot Natives. They set the village on fire. More than three hundred Pequot people died.

Only certain people could elect leaders. Some of the settlers did not like living there. They left Plymouth and moved south to Connecticut. They called their new home Windsor. It was the first lasting town in the state.

A Different Colony

Other people from the north came to the area. A minister named Thomas Hooker led a group of people. His group founded Hartford in 1636.

That year, Hartford joined with other towns to form the Connecticut Colony.

The people in the colony wrote a **charter**. It set up their government. At that time, most people could not choose their leaders. The charter said the people could now choose the leaders. The idea came from Thomas Hooker. Because of his good ideas, Hooker has been called "the father of Connecticut."

In 1660, the colonists wrote a new charter. This one said the people could elect a governor to lead the colony. It said they could make their own laws, too. The British king still ruled the colony. But he agreed to the new charter.

The next king did not like the charter. He named a

FACTS

What's in a Name?

Many Native people lived near the Connecticut River. They called their land *Quinnehtukqut*. The state takes its name from this Native word. It means "long river place" or "beside the long tidal river."

IN CONNECTICUT'S HISTORY

The Constitution State

Connecticut was the first colony to have a **constitution**. Later, people from the state helped write the U.S. Constitution. It was written at a meeting. Each state sent **delegates** to the meeting. At first, they could not agree on how to elect leaders. A Connecticut delegate named Roger Sherman had an idea that the others accepted. Now, Connecticut is called the "Constitution State."

new governor for the colony. This man went to Hartford to take back the charter. Someone hid the charter in an oak tree. The charter stayed safe, and the colony kept its government. Later, the oak tree was called the Charter Oak.

The Revolutionary War

By the 1770s, many of the American colonists

A few colonists from Connecticut signed the Declaration of Independence.

8

This mill was built in Connecticut in 1650. For many years, it used water power to grind corn.

Famous People of Connecticut

Harriet Beecher Stowe

Born: June 14, 1811, Litchfield, Connecticut

Died: July 1, 1896, Hartford, Connecticut

Harriet Beecher Stowe wrote many books. Her most famous book is *Uncle Tom's Cabin*. It was published in 1852. The book tells the story of African American slaves. Many people read her book. They learned how awful it was to be a slave. The book made many people in the South angry. But it helped convince others that slavery should end.

did not want British rule. They wanted to be free. Colonists began to fight the British. In 1775, the Revolutionary War started.

Connecticut supplied food, clothing, and guns

FUN FACTS

Yankee Doodle Dandy

During the Revolutionary War, British soldiers sang "Yankee Doodle Dandy." A British doctor in Connecticut wrote this song. The song made fun of colonial soldiers. They sang it anyway — and beat the British!

for the war. It also supplied soldiers. One soldier was Nathan Hale. He spied on British troops. The British caught him, and he was hanged. Before Hale died, he said these famous words: "I regret that I have but one life to lose for my country."

In 1783, the colonies won the war. They formed the United States of America. Connecticut became the fifth state in 1788.

From Farming to Factories

During the late 1700s, the state started to change. Its population grew. Factories sprang up along rivers. The rivers helped make power

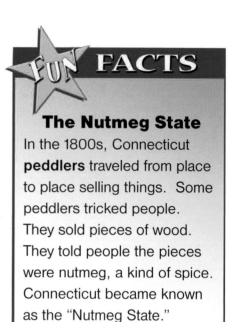

The Nutmeg State

In the 1800s, Connecticut **peddlers** traveled from place to place selling things. Some peddlers tricked people. They sold pieces of wood. They told people the pieces were nutmeg, a kind of spice. Connecticut became known as the "Nutmeg State."

that ran the factories. Boats on the rivers helped move goods. The factories made guns, hats, clocks, and other goods. Many of the people stopped farming and took jobs in the factories.

By the 1850s, Hartford had trains and steam-powered boats.

Hunting whales became a big business, too. Whaling ships left from Connecticut ports and returned with big sperm whales. People used whale oil to burn in lamps. They used whalebones to make umbrellas.

The Civil War

In the 1850s, states did not agree about slavery. Most Southern states wanted to keep slavery. Most Northern states wanted to end it. The Southern states broke away from the Northern states. They formed a new country called the Confederate States of America. In 1861, the South and the North started the Civil War.

Connecticut sent many soldiers to fight for the North. The state also made goods for the army. In 1865, the North won. Slavery ended, and the Southern states rejoined the Union.

From Factories to Suburbs

By the 1900s, more factories had been built. During World War I, they made guns and bullets. During

FUN FACTS

Connecticut Inventions

Many inventions have come from Connecticut. In 1793, Eli Whitney invented the cotton gin. This machine took the seeds out of cotton. It saved time and work. In 1836, Samuel Colt made a new kind of gun. Soldiers used this gun. It became very popular. A few years later, Charles Goodyear invented a way to make rubber tough. Then, rubber could be made into tires and other goods.

During World War II, the state made supplies for the war. In this picture, women sew clothes for the Air Force.

World War II, the factories made airplanes, submarines, and supplies.

After World War II, the state kept growing. More people lived in **suburbs**. Then, the state became a costly place to live and to do business. Factories left the state. They moved to places that were cheaper. The factory workers in Connecticut lost their jobs. Many could not find new ones. By the 1980s, many cities had thousands of poor people. Crime was a big problem.

Today, Connecticut has some of the nation's richest suburbs. It also has many poor people in its cities. The state is trying to fix its problems. It has bright, well-educated people. They can help lead the state into the future.

IN CONNECTICUT'S HISTORY

The Road to the White House

George H. W. Bush grew up in Connecticut. He was elected U.S. president in 1988. His son, George W. Bush, was born in Connecticut. Later, he went to college there. In 2000, he was elected president. He was reelected in 2004.

1614	Adriaen Block sails up the Connecticut River.
1636	Connecticut Colony is established.
1637	Colonists attack a Pequot village, killing more than three hundred Natives.
1776	The British execute Nathan Hale during the Revolutionary War.
1788	Connecticut becomes the fifth U.S. state.
1793	Eli Whitney invents the cotton gin.
1828	Noah Webster publishes the first American dictionary.
1852	Harriet Beecher Stowe publishes *Uncle Tom's Cabin*.
1861–1865	The Civil War is fought. Many Connecticut soldiers die in the war.
1954	The world's first nuclear submarine is launched from Groton.
1974	Ella Grasso is elected governor of Connecticut.
1988	George H. W. Bush is elected U.S. president.
2000	George W. Bush defeats Al Gore to become U.S. president. Gore's running mate is Joseph Lieberman, U.S. senator from Connecticut.
2004	The University of Connecticut men's and women's basketball teams both win national championships.

People

About 3.5 million people live in the state of Connecticut. It is growing slowly. Few people move to the state because it is a costly place to live.

Most people in the state live in or near cities. The largest city in the state is Bridgeport. Other big cities are New Haven and Hartford, the capital.

Many Kinds of People

Long ago, only Native Americans lived in Connecticut. Some groups of Native

Hispanics: In the 2000 U.S. Census, 9.4 percent of the people living in Connecticut called themselves Latino or Hispanic. Most of them or their relatives came from places where Spanish is spoken. They may come from different racial backgrounds.

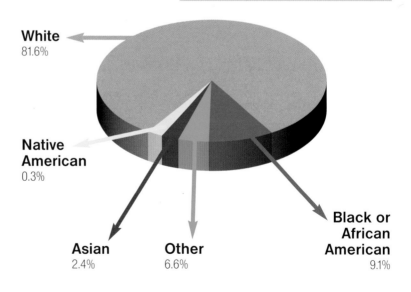

The People of Connecticut

Total Population 3,504,809

White 81.6%

Native American 0.3%

Asian 2.4%

Other 6.6%

Black or African American 9.1%

Percentages are based on the 2000 Census.

people moved away from their homes as the number of colonists grew. Other groups were wiped out in fights with colonists. Now, fewer than ten thousand Natives live in the state.

The first Europeans came from England. They settled in Connecticut in the 1630s. Two hundred years later, many more **immigrants** began to arrive. The first people to come were Irish. They took jobs in factories. They lived in Hartford and other cities. Next, Germans arrived. After the Civil War, people from England, Scotland, and Canada moved to the state. Other people came from Eastern Europe, Russia, and Italy, too. By the

Yale University is in New Haven. It has many old buildings.

early 1900s, seven out of ten people in the state were immigrants.

African Americans also moved to the state. Some came from the South after the Civil War. They worked on the state's tobacco farms. More arrived after World War II. Most of them lived in cities. In the last fifty years, many Hispanic people have moved to the state, too.

Religion and Education

Today, 85 percent of the people who live in the state are Christians. About half of the Christians are Catholics. Other Christians belong to Protestant churches. Other people in the state are Jews, Buddhists, Muslims, and Hindus.

Education always has been important in this state. Long ago, towns had to set up schools when they grew to a certain size. By the late 1800s, all children in the state went to school. Most of the schools were free.

This state has the highest percentage of people with college degrees in the nation. Many people attend one of the two state systems. These systems are the University of Connecticut and Connecticut State University. They have **campuses** all over the state.

Yale University is a famous private school. It is in New Haven. It was founded in the early 1700s. Other private schools in the state include Trinity College, in Hartford, and Wesleyan University, in Middletown.

Famous People of Connecticut

Ella Grasso

Born: May 10, 1919, Windsor Locks, Connecticut

Died: February 5, 1981, Hartford, Connecticut

Ella Grasso was the child of an Italian immigrant. In 1975, she became governor of Connecticut. She was the state's first female governor. She was the state's first Italian-American governor, too. Grasso was elected twice. She liked to get out and meet with people. She wanted to learn about their problems. Grasso also worked for equal rights for all people.

The Land

Connecticut has some flat land and some hilly areas. The flat land is in the Connecticut River Valley. This valley is in the center of the state. It has the state's best soil for farming. The land is also flat in the south, along Long Island Sound. Most of the big cities in the state are in these flat areas.

The northeastern and northwestern corners of the state have more hills. Part of the Taconic Mountains are in the northwestern corner. Most of these mountains are in New York and Massachusetts. The highest point in the state is 2,380 feet (725 meters) above sea level. It is on the

Boats travel on some parts of the Connecticut River. This part is near Long Island Sound.

CONNECTICUT

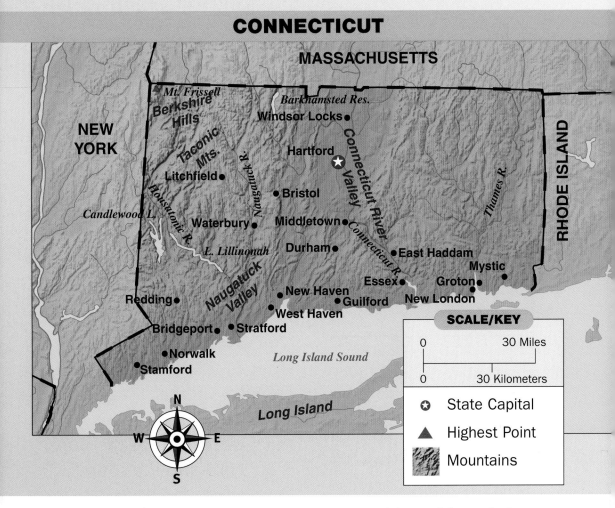

northwestern border of the state. This point is part of Mt. Frissell. The top of this mountain, however, is in Massachusetts.

Climate

Connecticut's weather is mostly mild. The winter is not terribly cold, and the summer is not very hot. Few ocean storms hit the state. Usually, the state's northern parts are colder than the southern parts. Sometimes, when snow falls in the north, the south gets rain.

FUN FACTS

The Leaf Season

Many people love the fall in Connecticut. During this season, many trees put on a show. Their leaves turn gold, red, and orange. **Tourists** travel to the state to see the trees. They come to enjoy the bright, beautiful colors.

Major Rivers

Connecticut River
407 miles (655 km) long

Housatonic River
148 miles (238 km) long

Naugatuck River
65 miles (105 km) long

Beaches, Rivers, and Lakes

The state's southern edge is on Long Island Sound. The sound is a long, narrow body of water. It is part of the Atlantic Ocean. It lies between Connecticut and Long Island, New York. Beautiful beaches line the sound. There are places to dock boats at many spots along the sound.

The state's longest river is the Connecticut River. It is the longest river in New England, too. It starts in New Hampshire and flows south. In Connecticut, it empties into Long Island Sound. Another long river is the Housatonic. It is in the western part of the state. It also flows to the sound.

These falls are on the Housatonic, the state's second longest river.

Connecticut has more than two thousand ponds and lakes. The largest is Candlewood Lake. This man-made lake lies in the western part of the state. Workers made a **dam** on the Housatonic River to create the lake. Many people swim and boat at this lake.

Plants and Animals

The state has great natural beauty. In spring, dogwoods bloom, showing off white or pink blossoms. Mountain laurel also blooms in the spring. It is the state flower. In fall, the leaves of some trees turn bright colors. These trees include birch, beech, elm, maple, and oak.

By the 1900s, many wild animals had disappeared from Connecticut. Early settlers hunted some types of animals for food and fur. They also cut down forests to make farms. Cutting down the forests destroyed the animals' homes. Wild animals became scarce. Today, however, they are coming back. The state has few farms now. More than half of the land is forested again. Deer, wild turkeys, and even a few moose live in the state. Foxes, coyotes, bobcats, and black bears live there, too.

FUN FACTS

A Dark Forest

Planes often fly between Boston and New York City. When they fly over most places on the East Coast at night, the pilots see bright lights below. When they fly over the northeastern part of Connecticut, pilots see nothing below. This part of the state has thick forests and few people. It looks completely dark!

Economy

Factories still provide many jobs in the state. Some make drugs for treating illnesses. Others make equipment for the U.S. military. They make submarines, aircraft parts, and helicopters.

Factories need a way to ship the goods they make. The state has excellent roads and highways. It has four railroads, too. Bridgeport and New Haven have ports for ships. Planes use Bradley International Airport, near Hartford.

The Insurance Capital

Hartford is a big center for insurance companies. People first sold insurance

This submarine base is in New London. In nearby Groton, submarines are made. Groton has been called the "submarine capital of the world."

there in the late 1700s. Today, it is home to fifty insurance companies.

Service Jobs

Many of the state's workers have service jobs. Doctors, lawyers, and teachers have service jobs. Many of the people who help tourists have service jobs, too. These service jobs include working in restaurants, hotels, and **casinos**.

Farming and Mining

Some people still work on farms. The state's biggest farm products are shrubs and flowers. Many farmers also sell eggs and milk.

Some companies sell crushed stone, gravel, and sand. They also mine for garnets. These stones are used in jewelry and in some kinds of machines that grind and cut.

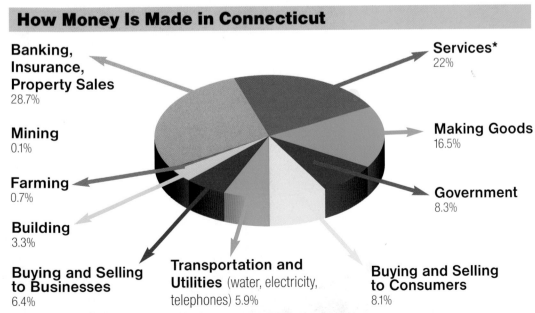

How Money Is Made in Connecticut

Banking, Insurance, Property Sales 28.7%

Services* 22%

Mining 0.1%

Making Goods 16.5%

Farming 0.7%

Government 8.3%

Building 3.3%

Buying and Selling to Businesses 6.4%

Transportation and Utilities (water, electricity, telephones) 5.9%

Buying and Selling to Consumers 8.1%

* Services include jobs in hotels, restaurants, auto repair, medicine, teaching, and entertainment.

Government

Hartford is the capital of Connecticut. The leaders of the state work there. The state government has three parts. They are the executive, legislative, and judicial branches.

Executive Branch

The executive branch carries out the state's laws. The governor heads this branch. The lieutenant governor helps the governor. Other **officials** also work in this branch. The governor chooses many of them. Others are elected.

Connecticut's capitol building is in Hartford. It was finished in 1879.

The inside of the capitol building has some beautiful woodwork.

Legislative Branch

Connecticut's legislative branch is called the General Assembly. It has two parts, or houses. They are the Senate and the House of Representatives. They work together to make laws for the state.

Judicial Branch

Judges and courts make up the judicial branch. They may decide whether people who have been accused of committing crimes are guilty.

Local Government

Connecticut has 169 towns and cities. Most towns are led by a group of elected officials. Most cities elect a mayor.

CONNECTICUT'S STATE GOVERNMENT

Executive		Legislative		Judicial	
Office	Length of Term	Body	Length of Term	Court	Length of Term
Governor	4 years	Senate (36 members)	2 years	Supreme (7 justices)	8 years
Lieutenant Governor	4 years	House of Representatives (151 members)	2 years	Appeals (9 judges)	8 years

Things to See and Do

I n Connecticut, many people like to have fun outdoors. They go to beaches on Long Island Sound. They visit lakes, too. They swim, boat, and fish. People also hike and camp in the forests.

Museums and More

People go to many museums in the state. New Haven and Hartford both have art museums. New Haven also has the Yale Peabody Museum of Natural History. The Beardsley Zoo is in Bridgeport. The Barnum Museum is there, too. It shows things about P. T. Barnum and his famous circus. The New England Air Museum is in Windsor Locks. It is the largest **aviation** museum in the northeast.

The state has quite a few historical sites. Some date back to the Revolutionary

Connecticut has many beaches.

26

War. Mystic Seaport looks like a whaling village from the 1800s. Visitors can board old sailing ships. In Essex, people ride an old steam train.

The state is home to two aquariums. The Mystic Aquarium has more than three thousand ocean creatures. The Maritime Aquarium in Norwalk has ocean life from Long Island Sound.

Theaters

Connecticut has fine theaters. The Long Wharf Theatre and Yale Repertory Theatre are in New Haven.

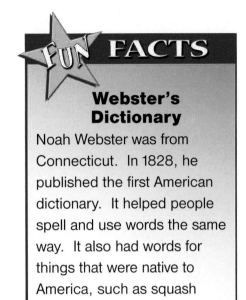

FUN FACTS

Webster's Dictionary

Noah Webster was from Connecticut. In 1828, he published the first American dictionary. It helped people spell and use words the same way. It also had words for things that were native to America, such as squash and skunks.

FUN FACTS

Nathan Hale Schoolhouses

Nathan Hale taught at two schools in Connecticut. Today, people can visit both of them. One is in East Haddam. The other is in New London.

Nathan Hale taught at this school, in New London. He also taught at a school in East Haddam.

The Goodspeed Opera House is in East Haddam. It was built in the 1800s. Shows often move from here to Broadway in New York City.

Festivals and Fairs

The state has many festivals and fairs. Guilford and Litchfield both have music festivals. New Haven and Mystic have arts festivals. Durham hosts a country fair. Hartford marks the life of writer Mark Twain.

Sports

Many people are Huskies fans. The Huskies play sports for the University of

Famous People of Connecticut

Joseph Lieberman

Born: February 24, 1942, Stamford, Connecticut

Joseph Lieberman grew up in Connecticut. In the 1970s, he served in the State Senate. He later served in the U.S. Senate. In 2000, he became the first Jew to run in a major party for U.S. vice president. He was Al Gore's running mate. Gore lost to George W. Bush. In 2000, Lieberman was reelected to the U.S. Senate.

Many people love to cheer for the Huskies. Below, the men's basketball team (white) plays a game. Both the men's team and the women's team were national champs in 2004.

Famous People of Connecticut

Mark Twain

Born: November 30, 1835, Florida, Missouri

Died: April 21, 1910, Redding, Connecticut

Mark Twain was born Samuel Langhorne Clemens. He grew up on the Mississippi River. Later, he became a writer. He used the name Mark Twain. In 1874, he moved to Hartford. There, he wrote *The Adventures of Huckleberry Finn* and other famous books. People still enjoy reading his books today.

Mark Twain once lived in this large house in Hartford. Today, it is open to visitors.

Connecticut. The men's and women's basketball teams have been very successful. The men were national champs in 1999 and 2004. The women's team has won the national championship five times. In 2004, both teams were champs! The men's soccer team won the national title in 2000.

The state is also home to the Connecticut Sun of the WNBA. Connecticut also hosts popular pro golf and tennis matches each year.

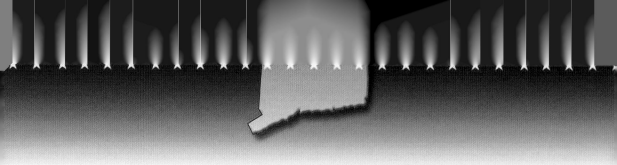

aviation — the making and flying of aircraft.

campuses — the places where a university or college is located

casinos — places where people can bet money while they play games

charter — a statement of rights and duties of a group of people

colony — a group of people living in a new land but controlled by the place they came from

constitution — a written document that creates a form of government and a set of laws

dam — a barrier built to slow down water flow

delegates — people who represent a group, state, or country at a meeting

factories — buildings where goods and products are made

immigrants — people who leave one country to live in another country

New England — a part of the northeastern United States made up of six states: Maine, New Hampshire, Vermont, Massachusetts, Rhode Island, and Connecticut

officials — people who hold important jobs in an organization, such as a government

peddlers — people who travel around selling goods

suburbs — areas outside of cities, made up mostly of homes

tourists — people who travel for fun

Books

The Colony of Connecticut. The Thirteen Colonies and the Lost Colony (series). Susan Whitehurst (PowerKids Press)

Connecticut. Rookie Read-About Geography (series). Susan Evento (Children's Press)

Connecticut Facts and Symbols. The States and their Symbols (series). Emily McAuliffe (Bridgestone Books)

Harriet Beecher Stowe. Mary Hill (Welcome Enterprises)

N Is for Nutmeg: A Connecticut Alphabet. Discover America State by State (series). Elissa D. Grodin (Sleeping Bear Press)

Nathan Hale. First Biographies (series). Christy Devillier (Buddy Books)

Web Sites

Connecticut Wildlife Division: Just for Kids Wildlife Page
dep.state.ct.us/burnatr/wildlife/learn/kids.htm

ConneCTkids
www.kids.ct.gov/kids/site/default.asp

Enchanted Learning: Connecticut
www.enchantedlearning.com/usa/states/connecticut

Mystic Seaport: The Museum of America and the Sea
www.mysticseaport.org

INDEX